Janusz Meyerhoff

MYTHS AND FACTS ABOUT THE FIRST TWO CENTURIES OF OUR ERA

CONTENTS

1) INTRODUCTION 1

2) PROLOGUE 3

3) WHAT HAPPENED BETWEEN
THE YEARS 5 BC AND 93 AD? 9

4) 93 AD. THE FIRST HISTORICAL
MENTION OF THE NAME
"JESUS CHRIST" 13

5)THE YEARS AFTER 93 AD 15

6) THE OLDEST NEW TESTAMENT
MANUSCRIPTS 17

7) BEGINNING OF CHRISTIANITY 21

8) EPISTLES 25

9) COMPARING JESUS TO OTHER
MYTHOLOGICAL FIGURES 27

10) FINAL REMARKS 29

INTRODUCTION

My interest in this subject dates from many, many years ago, just after the Second World War. At that time, I was in the Polish army, at the officer school in Rome, Italy.

Almost every week, a young Polish priest, who at that time was studying at the Vatican, used to visit us, giving informal chats. Although so many years have passed, I still remember them. They were about the beginnings of Christianity.

Much later, to my amazement, I found out that our lecturer became Pope John Paul II.

Lately, the fictional novel "Da Vinci Code" and the pseudo-documentary film "The Lost Tomb of Christ" awakened interest on this subject. However, many people took this fiction as historically true, and then many more works of fiction appeared — all absurd!

They mixed almost every myth possible: Jesus' son, Jesus' wife, Jesus' bloodline, The Holy Grail, The hidden treasure, The Templar Knights, the Masons, etc.

PROLOGUE

This inquiry, which I started to satisfy my own curiosity, can hurt the beliefs of many people. I am sorry, but I seek the truth only — I limit myself to what can be proven.

The reason for my pastime is to discover the real historical truth.

First, to discover the true history, we must make a distinction between prehistory and history.

What is that difference?

A) Prehistory (before writing appeared) is based on suppositions, legends, hearsay and unconfirmed reports. There can be some truth in it, or not...we may never know!

Memory transmitted orally, through many generations, by a professional storyteller, troubadour or minstrels, can be very deceptive, to say the least.

Usually they added to their stories: romance, fantastic creature, heroes, or diabolical beings. Sometimes they removed inconvenient information, or exaggerated some part of historical fact to make the story more attractive and more captivating for the audience.

In antiquity, storytellers were equivalent to today's historic film producers, which usually introduce into the historic motion picture romantic fairytales, or frightening creatures to enhance the true historic events.

It's a very well-known fact that the public wants fantasy, romance, heroes, violence, and horror, and the producer wants to satisfy them all, besides earning a lot of money.

Also, the memory passed orally by a family member cannot be trusted. Usually they were relating legends for the children and grown-ups, gathered during the long nights around a fireplace (no electric lights). They also were inclined to embellish, dramatize and exaggerate to keep their audience happy. It was an equivalent to today's entertainments like theatre, television, or cinema.

Also, we need to reflect on the fact that the more time elapsed between the historical event and the first written text, the less it should be trusted.

What do we know about the life of our forefathers who lived a few generations ago? — Nothing!

What do we know abut the life of our grandfather, who lives now? Surprisingly little!

So can we depend on the memory to know the true historical event? — NO!

Can we at least depend on infallible repeating?

During my adolescence, we used to play a curious game, "broken telephone." I assume that everybody knows it. However, I will try to explain.

Some ten kids, or more, were sitting in a row, one beside the other, like in a cinema; the first in a row whispered into his neighbor ear one word only; it could be anything. Then, in turn, each one had to repeat whispering the same word into his other neighbor's ear. The last one had to repeat that word loudly, so everybody could hear it.

It's amazing how distortions crept in after only a few repetitions. What the first kid whispered and what the last heard were always vastly different!

But, what does this kid's game have to do with the subject of history? Surprisingly quite a lot! This game was played in one room only and of course at the same time, and it's only repeating.

All stories, before being written, were based upon remembering and then repeating.

A person had to retain in his or her memory these stories for many years and then repeat them orally to the younger generation, which thinks differently and sometimes even has a different vocabulary.

Can we really depend on the veracity of these stories transmitted through many generations?

B) History is based on manuscripts and from objects found in excavations.

* Original manuscripts, or if it's impossible, reliable copies.

However, which manuscripts are truthful and which are not?

Even the original manuscript cannot be fully trusted. During antiquity, the same as now, many authors deformed, overstated or suppressed historic truth.

Also the copyists, sometimes by an error and sometimes on purpose, changed the original manuscript.

Just one extreme example: What would Roman history be like if it were based on Hollywood movies?

Also, the historic information comes usually from the winner's side, which shows only one side of the true history.

* Archeological artifacts found in excavations.

Having archeological objects (from ceramics, stone, wood, metals, or textiles) found in excavations makes the study of history easier and more precise. By knowing the exact place where the object was found, and by using new and advanced technologies, it is possible to deduce the lifestyle of these people, and even the history of the place.

The archeological excavations are the best and surest way to know a true and truthful history.

Nowadays, a big dilemma facing our civilization is the falsification of history.

And history is the memory of the society!

And, what is the purpose of memory?

Memory teaches us not to repeat mistakes and to duplicate successes! Therefore, when the historical account is erroneous, the lessons will be inadequate!

I found it necessary to include this lengthy explanation to show that many stories that we take for granted as being historically true are not; they are just fantasies and legends.

In the next chapters, I intend to show historical and confirmed scientific facts.

WHAT HAPPENED BETWEEN THE YEARS 5 BC AND 93 AD?

From this point forward, I will present all the facts in chronological order.

However, I must start the count five years before our era (5 BC) — Why?

In the sixth century AD, the monk, Dionysius Exiguus, established the year 1 AD as the year that Jesus was born. (Evidently it was an error.)

According to the calendar, king Herod died in year 4 BC, so Jesus must have been born, approximately, between the years 4 BC and 6 BC.

An example.

What is a historic event and what is not?

King Herod died in 4 BC. It is a historic event confirmed by many Roman documents.

However, King Herod's order to exterminate all newborns is not a historic event (it was written a long time after and nothing in history supports this story). Also, similar biblical stories can be found in many other ancient civilizations: for instance, Moses.

Amazingly, we have not a single Jewish, Greek, or Roman writer who ever mentioned Jesus during his lifetime.

Philo Judeaus (20 BC–50 AD). The greatest Jewish-Hellenistic philosopher and historian lived in the area of Jerusalem during the time of Jesus. Yet not once, in all of his volumes of writings, can we read a single account of a Jesus "The Christ."

Nor do we find any mention of Jesus, neither in Seneca's (4 BC–65 AD) writings, or from historian Pliny the Elder (23 AD–79 AD).

By accepted tradition, Jesus was born in the reign of Augustus, the great literary age of poets, orators and travelers. Yet not one single mention of the name of Jesus Christ was ever found.

All documents about Jesus were written well after his life.

The city of Nazareth is one of the oldest cities in the world. However, no evidence of a city of Nazareth, at the time of Jesus' life, exists. Nazareth ceased to be a city at around 6th century BC and then started to be populated again in the 2nd century AD.

Jesus Christ was supposedly crucified between the years 24 AD and 28 AD; however, no name of Jesus or Christ was found in Roman, Greek or Jewish manuscripts or in archeological evidence from that time.

Between the years 68 AD and 73 AD, the "Dead Sea scrolls" were deposited in the caves around Qumran, by Essen's, a Jewish religious sect. They are absolutely authentic and trustworthy.

The first scrolls were found by a Bedouin boy in the year 1947. Then many more scrolls, approximately 15.000 pieces, were found, many of them deteriorated. They are difficult to read and interpret.

Although many scientists worked and continue working on them, no mention of Jesus Christ was found. However, the "Dead Sea Scrolls" were written during the same period (between the 3rd century BC and 1st century AD) in the same place (around the Dead Sea) and also deal with religion — but nothing was discovered!

At that time, Christianity was probably an insignificant Jewish sect and not a worldwide religion.

The eruption of the Vulcan Vesuvius in the year 79 AD destroyed and covered with a layer of lava and dusts the cities of Pompeii and Herculaneum.

Almost three hundred years ago, the archeological excavations begun; however, until now, no inscription with the name of Jesus or Christ was found or any object belonging to the Christian religion.

Between the years 5 BC and 93 AD, no one has the slightest physical evidence to support a historical Jesus. Not a single object from the archeological excavations, no artifacts, no dwellings, no work of carpentry was found nothing.

93 AD - THE FIRST HISTORICAL MENTION OF THE NAME "JESUS CHRIST"

Famous Jewish writer Josephus in the tome XX of his book *Antiquitates Judaicae* refers to Jesus Christ.

This book of twenty tomes describes the history of Jewish people from creation until the revolt against Rome in then year 66 AD – 70 AD, and it was finished in the year 93 AD. So this famous paragraph was written in the year 93 AD, or a little before.

Josephus was Jewish by birth, but took the roman citizenship. He was hated by Jews, considered a traitor, resided in Rome, was vain and egocentric. However, his books give an invaluable testimony of that époque, but cannot be believed as he was unreliable and often changed and distorted historic facts.

In the tome XVIII of *Antiquitates Judaicae*, there is another mention of Christ. However, it was an obvious and posterior tampering by a Christian copyist.

Falsification is nothing new!

So at least seventy years had passed between Jesus' life and the first written manuscript describing his life.

Therefore, The New Testament cannot be taken as a historically accurate account, only as hearsay stories transmitted through many generations...

THE YEARS AFTER 93 AD

The roman writer TACITUS was born in the year 64 AD and his book ANNALS (tome XV, sec. 44), written approximately in the year 109 AD, briefly mentions the name "Christ."

Also TACITUS describes the big fire that destroyed the city of Rome in the year 64 AD when the emperor Nero started the persecution of Christian sects, which he did not clearly distinguish from Jewish sects, blaming them for starting the fire.

However, not a single writer, of the emperor Nero period, ever mentioned Jesus or Christianity, and TACITUS wrote this description fifty-five years after the big fire.

SUETONIUS, Roman historian and writer, born in 69 AD, mentioned the name "Chrestus" in his book written in the year 109 AD.

THE OLDEST NEW TESTAMENT MANUSCRIPTS

Probably the oldest portion of a New Testament manuscript is a small papyrus fragment of the gospel of John housed in the John Rylands University library in Manchester, England, dated to 100–125 AD. However, in recent decades some developments and debates have been going on, which eventually can move papyrus 52 out of its place as the oldest surviving New Testament fragment.

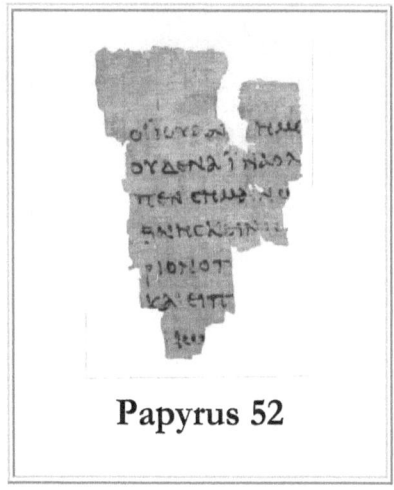

Papyrus 52

The three small fragments of a papyrus 64 of the gospel of Matthew currently are in the Magdalene College library in Oxford, and dated around the late 200 AD.

However, the debates about the exact dating are still going on.

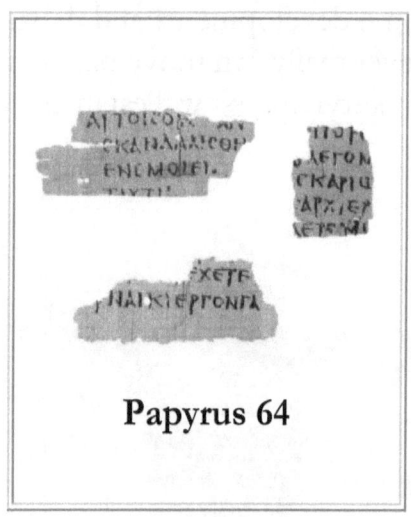

Papyrus 64

Codex Vaticanus

Codex Vaticanus (currently in Vatican), which dates from the 4th century AD, and Codex Sinaiticus (currently in the British Library in London), which also dates from the 4th century AD, are the oldest excellent parchments of the entire New Testament.

Of course, both these Codex's were copies of previous copies.

The Codex is written in ancient Greek.

How do we know that these manuscripts are so old?

We can date papyrus manuscripts by looking at the way they were written. Handwriting is always developing and differences are bound to appear. An expert, a paleographer, cannot establish the exact date but he can give us a rough estimation. However, for an ancient period as that between 100 AD and 300 AD, it is much more difficult to be confident about the date of a manuscript.

Of course, we can establish an exact age of existing copies by using the carbon 14 method.

BEGINNING OF CHRISTIANITY

After the year 110 AD, a flood of various texts with the description of the life of Jesus Christ began — many of them contradictory.

Therefore, Irenaeus (influential father of the early Christian church), who lived in the second part of the 2nd century AD, discarded most of them and chose four gospels: Mark, Luke, Matthew and John. These four gospels became cannons for the Christian faith. We do not know who wrote them, as none of the gospels were written during Jesus' life. Neither any author of gospel claimed to meet a living Jesus.

All others gospels, called Apocrypha's, were declared heretical, burned, destroyed or lost.

However, later on, many more heretical manuscripts were found again. Most of them belonged to Gnostic sects.

Most Biblical historians consider that the New Testament was originally written in the second part of the first century AD. But no original manuscripts, neither copies from that period, were found. Besides dating by paleographers, no other scientific proof exists.

The Christian church has depicted the authors of gospels as disciples of Jesus. But consider…if the birth of the writer of the gospel occurred at about the same time as

Jesus' birth, that would make John to be 110 years old when he wrote his gospel.

Also, between Jesus' crucifixion and the writing of gospels, there is a gap of a few generations...and we know that orally transmitted stories are not trustworthy.

In 1945, an Arab made an archeological discovery in Egypt of several papyruses. They have been referred to as the *Nag Hammadi* texts, and contain fifty-two heretical books that include gospels of Thomas, Philip, James, John, and many others. Archeologists have dated them at around 350–400 AD. They are copies from previous copies, and none of the original texts exist. Some scholars think that original manuscripts were written around 120–150 AD.

Later on, another copy of a manuscript, Gospel of Judas, was found in Egypt...It's also from around the 4th century AD and was written in Coptic. The original Greek version probably dates around 130–170 AD. This Gospel tells of Judas as the most loyal disciple, just the opposite of the canonical gospels.

The gospels describe stories written in the third person. But people who are eyewitnesses will write in the first person. Therefore, gospels are hearsay accounts.

EPISTLES

Paul's (Paul of Tarsus) biblical letters (epistles) serve as the oldest surviving Christian texts, and were probably written around 60 AD. However, this dating is not reliable. Thirteen epistles are attributed to Paul, but his authorship of six epistles is questioned by some scholars.

There is not a single occurrence that he ever met or saw a real Jesus. Therefore, all stories about Jesus could have come from other followers or from his imagination… Hearsay accounts.

Epistles of James: Gospels mention many deferent James…Which one of them?

Epistle of James refers to Jesus only once and there is no indication of historical Jesus. Many scholars consider the epistle to be written in the late first or early second centuries.

What eliminates it from being a historical account?

Epistles of John: The Epistle of John, the Gospel of John, and Revelation are so different in style and content that they could not come from the same author. So we don't know who wrote these epistles and anyway the Epistle of John says nothing about seeing a historical Jesus. Therefore, they can serve only as hearsay descriptions.

Epistles of Peter: The first Epistle of Peter is addressed to various churches in Asia Minor, suffering from religious persecution. Estimates for the date of composition range from 75 to 112 AD. At least four generations have passed between Jesus' life and writing of this epistle. So they can serve as unconfirmed accounts only. Also, many scholars question the authorship of Peter.

In all epistles, there are no eyewitness accounts of a historical Jesus and were written many generations after Jesus' life. Therefore, all of them serve as hearsay accounts.

COMPARING JESUS TO OTHER MYTHOLOGICAL FIGURES

There is no doubt that Christian mythology bears a striking resemblance to many myths of legendary heroes of various ancient religions.

Above all, the Herculean myth resembles Jesus in many areas.

Hercules gets born as a human from union of God (Zeus) and the mortal and chaste Alcmene, his mother.

Similar to King Herod who wanted to kill Jesus, Hera wanted to kill Hercules.

Hercules traveled the earth as a mortal helping mankind and performed miraculous deeds.

Hercules died, rose to mount Olympus and became a god.

People in Ancient Greece and Rome believed that he actually lived, told stories about him, worshipped him, and built temples to him.

The pre-Christian cult of Mithra had a deity of light and truth,

Fought against evil,

Had the burial in a rock tomb,

Believed in resurrection,

Had the sacrament of bread and water,

Performed marking on the forehead with a mystic mark.

All well before the advent of Christianity.

The Egyptian mythical Horus, god of light and goodness, resembles Jesus in many areas.

Horus and the Father (Osiris) are one

Horus, the Father seen in the Son

Horus, light of the world

Horus was baptized with water by Anup

Horus was the Good Shepherd

Horus with the Tat Cross

The Trinity of Atum, the Father — Horus, the Son — Ra, the Holy Spirit.

Horus, as eternal life

Twelve were the followers of Horus.

The Greek, Roman, Egyptian, Persian and pagan mythologies were closely similar to the Jesus mythology. Dozens of similar savior stories propagated the minds of humans long before the life of Jesus.

FINAL REMARKS

The topic of this small booklet deals with an extremely controversial subject. The profound abyss that separates science from faith...it's impossible to traverse.

However, it's nothing new. For instance: the interpretation of the Bible by Catholic Christianity placed our earth at the center of the universe.

It took many years and many victims (usually burned at the stake by the inquisition), to displace our planet from this elevated position.

No original book of the New Testament survives. What we have are copies, and copies of copies of questionable originals. Maybe, even if the stories came gradually over time, then the original texts may have never existed.

The whole quandary is the fact that there is no actual proof of Jesus' life...in the whole of the New Testament, no eyewitness accounts for historical Jesus occurs.

www.ingramcontent.com/pod-product-compliance
Lightning Source LLC
Chambersburg PA
CBHW061233280526
45784CB00006B/2746